LITTLE STRANGER

Books by Lisa Olstein

Little Stranger

Lost Alphabet

Radio Crackling, Radio Gone

Lisa Olstein

LITTLE STRANGER

COPPER CANYON PRESS
PORT TOWNSEND, WASHINGTON

Cover art: Fred Tomaselli, *Birds and Trees,* 1996. Photo collage, acrylic,
gouache, leaves, and resin on wood panel, 48 x 48 in (121.92 x 121.92 cm).
© Fred Tomaselli/Courtesy James Cohan Gallery, New York/Shanghai.

Copper Canyon Press is in residence at Fort Worden State Park in Port
Townsend, Washington, under the auspices of Centrum. Centrum is a gather-
ing place for artists and creative thinkers from around the world, students
of all ages and backgrounds, and audiences seeking extraordinary cultural
enrichment.

LIBRARY OF CONGRESS CATALOGING-IN-PUBLICATION DATA
Olstein, Lisa, 1972–
Little stranger / Lisa Olstein.
pages cm
ISBN 978-1-55659-432-8 (pbk. : alk. paper)
I. Title.

PS3615.L78L58 2013
811'.6—DC23

2012051259

987654342 FIRST PRINTING

COPPER CANYON PRESS

Post Office Box 271
Port Townsend, Washington 98368
www.coppercanyonpress.org

Acknowledgments

Thank you to the editors of the journals where poems from this collection, sometimes in earlier versions or under different titles, first appeared.

Crosscurrents Review, "The Brain Is an Operations Center," "Cold Satellite," "Elegy (we see how the children cluster)," "Themselves Performing Small Brave Acts," "This Season It's All about 3D"

Event, "My Eyes Were Harbors," "To Where"

Fou, "Necessary Monsters"

Fourteen Hills, "Was to Have Been Called Whip-Poor-Will"

Free Verse, "Smaller Devices," "I'm Writing You a Telegraph and the Pony and the Pony Express Man Are Waiting by the Door," "Silver Whips of Trees"

Glitterpony, "Different Habitats Make for Good Neighbors," "Furniture Music," "This Waking Life"

Indiana Review, "Control Group," "A Mr. and Mrs. Rajik Once Existed and Lived Happily in Kalisz"

jubilat, "Teaching Farm," "This Is a Test of the Internal Emergency Broadcast System"

Medaille Prelude, "Helpmeet, Handmaiden"

Narrative Magazine, "Aubade," "Deserter's Information Center," "Space Junk," "When You're a Top Predator You Have to Survive," "You Can Tell a Tiger by Its Stripes"

The Nation, "Ibex Have Evolved for Life at the Top"

Polutona Magazine, "Aubade," "Space Junk" (in Russian translation)

Women's Studies Quarterly, "Every Boy, Every Blood"

A number of poems from this collection appear in anthologies, installations, or other projects; thank you to the editors, curators, and collaborators.

"Cold Satellite" and "Deserter's Information Center" comprise lyrics to songs of the same names that appear on the album *Cold Satellite,* released by Jeffrey Foucault and Cold Satellite in 2010 (US) and 2011 (Europe). "Elegy (in a distant room)," "Every Boy, Every Blood," "Necessary Monsters," and "Silver Whips of Trees" comprise lyrics to songs of the same names on *Cavalcade,* released by Jeffrey Foucault and Cold Satellite in 2013.

"This is a Test of the Internal Emergency Broadcast System" and "Space Junk" appear in *The New Promised Land: 120 Contemporary Jewish American Poets,* eds. Deborah Ager & Matthew Silverman, Continuum Books, 2013.

"A Tiger's Roar Is Friend" appears in *Morning Song: Poems for New Parents,* eds. Susan Todd & Carol Purington, St. Martins Press, 2011.

"Marooned" appears in *The Hero with a Thousand Faces,* a limited-edition chapbook featuring collages by Lily Perreira paired with responsive poems by various poets.

"Control Group" is part of *The Poetry Dress,* a collaborative art project culminating in an installation by Danielle Jones-Pruett.

Several poems' titles originated in a title-sharing project with Heather Christle. Shared titles include: "Diorama," "Themselves Performing Small Brave Acts," and "This Waking Life." The title "Was to Have Been Called Whip-Poor-Will" is a phrase borrowed from Edward Hopper's notebook. The titles of the poems in section two are phrases excerpted from diorama captions at the Field Museum in Chicago.

Thank you to the Sustainable Arts Foundation for its generous support. Thank you Jeffrey, Goody, Billy, Alex, Jeremy, Justin, and Hayward for the beautiful alchemy. Thank you Kris for irreplaceable, irrepressible companionship down all the many paths. Thank you Michael for bottomless generosity and insight. Thank you Noy, Rob, Matthea, Heather, and Betsy for essential encouragement and advice. Thank you Rick and Ashley for use of The Lookout. Thank you to my parents, whose love and support make everything possible. Thank you to Kelly, Joseph, Tonaya, and everyone at Copper Canyon Press.

for David & for Toby

Contents

*

*

*

LITTLE STRANGER

*

Themselves Performing Small Brave Acts

Books tell us how to pierce the neck,
how to open the airway of a fellow passenger
with a hollow pen, how to wrestle an alligator,
but not how to out-swim a bear.

There's no out-swimming a bear.
Books tell us about men on mountaintops
who freeze without ever putting on
the extra sweaters in their packs,

who starve with food in their pockets,
poor bastards, they tell us how not to be like them.
We bring ourselves to very cold places
so we may feel warmer when we huddle inside.

We admire the raptors that live in our city,
a city we'd thought unfit for the wild,
the way they soar above traffic and make nests
of pylons and still manage to find trees.

We admire the way they wait for mates
no one believes will ever come
and the way they mate, and the way they wait
for a new mate when the old one suddenly is gone.

Spirit Level

Star of our morning séance,
the river rises up out of itself:
ectoplasm of mist, body above body
sliding between shores.
Geese line up as if the field
runs in strict corridors.
We are a negligible riverbank feature,
eyes behind binoculars, we carry
no rifles, we are easily ignored.
People jog slowly down our street.
They glide by with cameras,
in striped racing gear, on many-geared
bicycles, back and forth from the store.
I am hopeful, and the hopeful seek
the hopeless, a level always
in need of rising. In this way
I distill the world to the push-pull
between us, our battleground is
a perfect microcosm, we don't
need to leave the house anymore.
In flight, wings look like they are waving.
Everything around us says I am
changing while to one another we say,
I can't hear what you're saying.

This Is a Test of the Internal Emergency Broadcast System

On her way home from school
your little girl wants spotted mice
from the pet store.

She wants to give them a bath
without losing them in the suds
but they escape their paper bag

and disappear underfoot in the car.
Now your little girl wants
a bright green snake

that won't get lost in the snow.
The red-tipped posts lining
the drive look wounded.

This is not an emergency.
This is winter saying, I decapitated
your small glass bird.

Hungry deer step from the woods
on velvet-gloved legs.
This is a test.

Place your elevated heart
rate in this prepaid, self-addressed,
steel envelope.

We should all be prepared
to proceed calmly
through the crackling air.

Teaching Farm

They put a plug in the cow
to stop the hole they carved in its flank
for recruits to plunge their arms into
feeling for spoons and pasture debris.
Mulch accomplishes what?
Insulates the brains of dormant tubers.
Moss accomplishes what?
Salves the edges of jagged stones
the dog will not fetch.
The dog is fierce out of fear,
the instructor says, holding a cloth
to the deliveryman's bleeding leg.
Everyone's crying from the pepper
spray that misfired in the wind.
They all carry it now plus biscuits.
We stand around on a field of fiery green
squares thick with researched seed.
The field looks like a pinwheel
to the balloonist floating the near sky.
It's his first time and he thought it'd be more
peaceful but the gas keeps firing
and he can't control the drift of his glide.
It's like the air is arguing all around him
and he really doesn't care what we have for dinner
as long as we can sit down and eat.

Blood, Bread, Spoons

Can we agree there's no such thing
as a "gustnado" despite the local
headlines, but in strong winds
we're right to be afraid and no,
the tobacco barn does not belong
in the middle of the road?
Definitions only matter insofar as
they matter or actually predict
the future, as in gale-force,
metastatic, foreclosed.
We admire them, we collect them
in hopes of expanding our small,
tired stables of words, but mostly
we don't, smirking at each other's
attempts at tergiversation, oneiric.
What's the matter with dreamy
and who do you think you are
anyway, the Queen of England?
The Queen of England moves always
through a cloud of definitions:
who may touch her (no one),
how she may touch (as if she feels nothing).
She looks lonely in the solemn crowd
of her hat and its small veil,
her gloved fingers and so many
measured distances. So what
if she eats the people's gold
for breakfast? It's the only thing
her stomach understands.

Control Group

Blind babies smile on the same
schedule as those with sight.

Consumers will pay more
for leather made from the skin

of an animal never bitten by mosquitoes.
Either the mute child spoke

in full sentences alone in the dark
or the monitors picked up ghosts

of pelicans streaming over the bridge.
A solitary locust may seem far

removed from a depressed person.
Mice are the second most successful

mammal. A monkey on board
a Jupiter AM-18 rocket is a hero.

Miss Baker. A monkey in a cage
is a number. In the wild,

the only way to separate a monkey
from her infant is to kill her.

In this next experiment, your child
is kidnapped and broadcast

back to you on a wide, flat screen,
an orphan crying himself to sleep in the dirt.

#433 hangs from her mother's tit
while one cage over her twin #434

throws his body against the bright
steel walls of his enclosure.

Deserter's Information Center

The flags on Main Street say
you are one, are you one of us?
They hang in the exhalation
of three thousand people sleeping,
breathing deeply, eyes whirring,
coding messages, shedding messages,
the night before a parade.
Coyotes are lying down in their dens.
The nest of phoebes has not yet woken.
Corn repeats itself into a haze
of tassels and sheaving leaves.
Autumn sharpens its knives.
No more movies hung on sheets
in the park, in the school parking lot,
until next year. Next year.
Your children will become unrecognizable.
They will love a picture of you
more than you every time you speak.
The smell in the hall will migrate
back and forth between memories,
behind doors: substitute ghost
once again waiting, once again come.

Furniture Music

During the first snowstorm
we busy ourselves with wind

and the torque of falling
flakes. During the second

we watch menageries
slipping past our windows.

After the fourth we stay inside.
We grow accustomed to

our solitude. We grow hungry.
By the sixth we eat only

what's white. We watch deer
teeter on teacup hooves.

If we thought about leaving
the house we'd be terrified.

We think instead of polar bears
patient on ice floes breathing

into the breathing holes where
seals surface, the frigid air

where their mouths won't quite meet.
We think of the famous Siberian

tiger in the zoo pacing while
perfect camouflage accumulates.

To Where

I am a girl. Every morning
I choose carefully how to dress,
but I like it best when
my clothes don't matter.
Where I live, it is still cold.
Are you pockmarked by winter?
Is pockmarked a word
you've ever heard before?
What is your favorite time of day?
What is your favorite thing
about morning? If you have slept
for many days, when you wake,
does it feel like morning no matter
what time it is? When you are
very hungry, do you eat too fast?
If you found me picking berries,
would you brush me aside
or would you carry me off somewhere?
Do you think about problems
while you sleep? Sleeping is
when bones grow. Sleeping is
to love the dark. I love it so much
I want to be it, for a while,
then I wake up. Did you know
that dolphins sleep with half their brains?
Because of breathing.
Because of sharks.
Because they are mammals
but water is their home.
Have you been pulled asleep
from your home and put back
near to where you were but not exactly?
Did it seem like a dream?

The Brain Is an Operations Center

The raccoon in the good-enough woods
knows when to expect you.

The geese don't look down
from diagramming the sky.

Suddenly the boy is scared of coyotes,
worried for his cartoon animal friends.

Your body is wired through the air to his body.
Like a sharpshooter who knows to pull the trigger

between heartbeats, you can test-run
the system in your mind. There is

a blankness shame will fill but for now
there is only one way to feel: afraid.

Necessary Monsters

The bullet the horse
fears most is the one
on its back so it drives
a twisting course through
the storm of the night.
The heart inside the brain
throbs, tiny pain center,
tiny command post
inside an ocean swimming.
No maps here, barely yet
a maze, cells burning,
no scent of fig in the fig
tree's branches, not yet
any tree. In the distance
the city is a dappled ruby
hub, ruby mouth, harbor
in its teeth. Fine lines mark
the eyes, lace the air,
might be features, might be
lookout posts, might be far-off
lamplight tulips soldiers
step from into the shallows,
their steady horses prancing
up the angled plank pointing
to the ship pointing to the sea,
not yet the sea, the shallows
churn, the shallows sway, not
yet, when do we say the sea?

*

A Tiger's Roar Is Friend

At last the cedar waxwings
come in late April rain
for the pagoda tree's seeds
that have hung slack all winter
and once again begin to swell.
A mallard roots with her orange beak
a puddle by a busy walkway,
trading the overcrowded pond
for a site more dangerous still.
The T'ang dynasty second period
veil of the day is impenetrable.
Beneath the sky cage of my ribs,
a son practices breathing.

Different Animals

Now when I collide with you
we will both stay our separate selves.
Beautiful experimental techniques
show that this is so. Surveys
made with trains and shattered glass.
With dogs and tiny spoons.
We press our ears all night to each
other's ears. We wake to frost
and fire-smoke drifting. We wake
to bees in the frills of cherry trees.
We are beakers emptied and refilled.
The price of gold is rising, but
gold is of no use to us. We wake
to the sound of the sea in our ears,
our own or each other's, we're not sure.

Ibex Have Evolved for Life at the Top

When we say *specimen*
we mean you. By *you*
we mean whatever
collection of night sweats
and shopping lists accumulates
in the bed by dawn. When
we say *dark* we mean pitch,
moonless, starless,
don't even open your eyes.
When we say *he has your eyes*
we mean we see nothing
of you there. If you want
someone to come for you,
you'll have to cry harder than that.
If you want to be prepared,
practice: blizzard, fire, famine.
Your shoes or your coat?
Your cat or your dog?
Sister, daughter, mother, wife?

Barasingha Find Safety in Numbers

Sleep deprivation is a form of torture
leading to insanity. All parents are
sleep deprived, anguished victims
of their own desire. I know this
has been said before but I can't
remember where. Dissociation
and identity confusion are
the first to strike. A new mother
who says her baby sleeps through
the night is deranged. She is
suckling a sickly button quail.
You should not be the one to tell her.
Elation may be just another form
of fear. If water can be just another
kind of air. There's nothing irrational
about a parasite. Darling, the beauty
of your Cheerios haunts me,
appearing at the center of my fist,
dropping from my hair.

Notes from the Wilderness

Shh is the one sound
allowed into the vacuum-
sealed laboratory because
this is what a door says
when it is opened or closed.
We pinch the mist
where it branches.
We seed cloud forests
on the banks of cloud seas.
Beneath a blanket of moon,
waist-high, elbow-deep—
this is our only method.
We measure by eye,
eyes shut, until we hear a cry.
We are unkissed for years
by the sun. Colors pool
and pass through us.
When we are nearly translucent.
When we can no longer see
our milk-white hands.
Then the real work begins.

You Can Tell a Tiger by Its Stripes

Baby plays in the tub with a net
and paddle toys. Swimmy frog
wins for speed. Swimmy dog
wins for distance, for persistence,
he will not stop. Sometimes
picking things up and putting them
down is enough. Baby says, *don't*
call me baby I'm fourteen
get out of the fucking bathroom please.
No, not yet, but the future is a scent
on the breeze that brings air
from the place you're heading.
A certain amount of fear is perfect
is the startle that brings the relief
that brings the laughter that rights the room.
A certain amount is suddenly too much.
After surprise comes deception,
the eureka moment, you are a shell gamer
and I am a shell gamer, too.
Watch this dog disappear, this frog.
Watch this baby.

Heavy Hunters Rely on Stealth

I fell in love anew.
He was an invention:
two parts rabbit in winter,
one part hawk above the koi pond.
Physics were involved
and the baring of nests by trees.
I knelt and his face drifted by me,
cirrus, cumulus, nimbus,
a moon full of named and frozen seas.
Kiss me in darkness, kiss me in light,
I seemed to be saying,
stupidly, while it rained.

When You're a Top Predator You Have to Survive

Careful, there's a boy attached to that string.
His invisible swan is meticulous about its feathers
and now the rain is here in angles.
Although adept at sensing vibrations like schooling fish,
a child requires his own intimate instigation of terror.
He will look with wonder and no alarm
from the dog's dancing tail to his playmate's
panicked shrieking then back again
to the tallest mountains always turning out to be
clouds spooling and unspooling their thread.

Sambar Lead Private Lives

On a steamer it's always somebody's job
to steer. Trapped fish lie down
so no water moves through them.
In the wild only the alpha wolves mate.
The rest of the pack watches and waits.
I refuse to estimate how many times
I've unlocked these doors. Here's one way
to know you're home: stop counting.

Leopards Are Flexible Cats

When the dentist tells me
he's found a remnant of a baby tooth
hiding alongside my right bicuspid,
I'm born again: eight years old
and bleeding happily beneath
the apple tree, bicycle a small wreck
in the distance, clover light
and eye spots filling the screen.
This is how we know the world:
hit something hard, hit something soft,
sit by a glowing window and watch
the lighted storm swim by.

I'm Writing You a Telegraph and the Pony and the Pony Express Man Are Waiting by the Door

Silked and tassled, the cornfield glows
a rose halo meadowlarks stitch

to the steaming ground. I come to you
in need. We both accept this.

We make fewer and fewer distinctions
between what is said and unsaid,

what we meant by what we said before.
Something like a breeze is billowing

our figurative skirts, our figurative sails,
unnamed things are leaving us,

we feel it in the ankles, at the shoulders,
as soon as we leave the shore.

We mark each passing with nothing,
we regret arrivals and departures

by equal score. A firefly lands, ghost
messages in green. Campfire body, burn.

Cold Satellite

In the second chamber
of my fourth heart
down to the left of the third valve
is the room I keep for you
for me to think of you.
It's where I find you drowsy,
half-asleep, half-clothed,
with your eyes half-closed.
Lace the curtains with holes,
you say, let me out.
This is no room at all,
why don't you mix me a fucking drink,
you say, or draw me a map
but all I hear is beating.
A satellite passes every three hours
and thirty-three minutes
through our night-blackened sky.
It sees the world in a ribbon's width
blindly with steel eyes
and waves that read the air
that write the air we can't read.

Marooned

Everybody's got a story he said
I've been raped
I've been dead
I've been a criminal
I've been all of the above
he said you need an angle
bull and steer are simple biology
but oxen are made by the work
they turn their bodies to
it takes years he wanted me to know
it takes patience he's been talking
like this since Topeka and I'm wearing
the dress the rain suggested
but my timing is off
sun breaks the world into seeds
seeds into words words into
some flowers are all fire
and how many moons lumber
across the daytime sky Mother
is that you your thousand fingers
glistening like drawbridges
narrowing like planks
there's something wrong
under the hood he says here
take this map he says to the dog
in me he thinks just wants to
bring her master a morsel
but what I want is a lake
to hit me in the face the pooled
distance every shortcut shaved
and this map reads like a score
and no wind is my conductor

The Flow of Alien Deer

All borders are treacherous.
All crossings are sewn with small steps.

Invisible walls don't harm us
until we're hit in the face.

There's something we long for
like peepers for their calling

all night during their season of calling.
There's something we hope for

like a child hopes to be chosen.
When the ear and the eye compete,

the eye wins. When hunger and fear,
hunger. When memory, desire.

Exile the Dragon-Tailed and the Rabbit-Eared among You

There is a queen peeking
from your bedroom window
as if a terrace, as if a crowd.
Nobody notices her waving
in the dark. She didn't ask for this
life. Yellow was chosen for her
six hundred years ago during
a short truce in a long war.
Every dog I ever loved just died,
say her eyes as the eyes of every
dead dog I ever loved stare back at me
from the windowsill and earlier
at the checkout counter as the clerk
explained how carefully he crushed
between two spoons the pills
into a fine powder, stirred them
into a bowl of meat and carried Pal
outside for one last meal. Maybe
you're in trouble, says the queen.
Maybe you don't need a lover.
Maybe you're a thousand ways broken.

Dear Sir

Dear Sir:

No one can see it, but I feel it,
against my skin, silky disease
beneath my clothes. Like stones
in a stream my dreams turn over
and you are beneath every one.
What is your advice to me?

Dear Sir:

Dissatisfaction dresses me
according to its own schedule.
Sometimes I imagine you
sitting beside me. When
the trace of someone's scent is left
on my skin, like a car crash
suddenly you're there.

Dear Sir:

It was a lot of provisions to waste,
but the need to stop and think of you
was overpowering. You are
the slippery side of the road
when the rain comes part way down.
You are the midnight mountain
against the midnight sky. Today
I watched a hawk soar against
a background of no clouds hunting
pigeons. The horses appear larger
in the snow. They know to fear
their ribbon fences.

Dear Sir:

Today the horses ignored me.
The blue-eyed pony is companion
to the nervous mare but his spirit
is mean. I sort the hours
like colored beads. My breath
is a pulley. My eyes work together
but they are not friends.

Dear Sir:

The heightened awareness,
the grace the senses bring
to the landscape, to the beloved
before imminent departure,
this is where I reside.
The day's tasks fill up,
they blossom with you.
You are a dogged pursuit
and I am a dog, trembling.
If you open your hand,
I'll rub myself against it.

With these pits beneath my tongue.
These kittens in my teeth.

Dear Sire:

I understand the desired
is also desire, that every you
is you, that what we want is
a container for many wishes.
Sometimes I let the room grow
dark around me. It has only
ever been fleeting, satisfaction
with the friend I am given.
As if each embrace is a trigger
I pull just to find the wish to stop.

Dear Siren:

To whom are you making these declarations?
Do you hear me not listening,
not imagining my fingers in your hair?
Stop speaking to me in code. I tried
to love each day on its treasonous march
forward. It's too late. It'll be months
before the light shines this sideways again.

Dear Sir:

I would take no pills
but I need them. At night
I lie down flat like a river
waiting for its blanket of birds.

*

Was to Have Been Called Whip-Poor-Will

The hero is tall.
The heroine is seated.
They gaze in different directions.
Behind them, the trees
in phalanx formation
creeping up on one another
in the dark. They're here
for the last of the sunlight,
angled, lit from below.
In his ears, war, the last
things he heard: fire and cries,
people like matchsticks,
fuel for bonfires, loud
growing muffled as if
behind a curtain of snow.
In her eyes, a father,
a forest, a girlhood girded
by snow. In the bay,
periscopes like birds' necks,
like cormorants searching
the shore. Dog hears it.
It will be there out of sight.
In the trees creeping
through the oil-slick dark.
Dog hears it, whip-poor-will,
hears hill, hill, and then the sea,
and then the sea.

A Mr. and Mrs. Rajik Once Existed and Lived Happily in Kalisz

Dusk slid like a finger
down a spine. A fine-
needled pine. The woods
were full of them.
Sometimes sadness,
sometimes joy. Lovers
slipped past lovebirds
in decorative cages.
Ambassadors monitored
their regular tables,
their heavy wooden
doors. Uniforms at first
are rarely frightening.
Uniforms at first hum
a quiet song. A parrot
might preen your eyelashes
but to even the best
trained falcon you are only
ever a pocket lined with meat.

Helpmeet, Handmaiden

Forgive me, but holding down your arms
while someone else pins your legs
and the makeshift nurse probes your wound,

while she curses and somewhere bells ring
and the commotion of tools falling
surrounds us, is the best that I can do.

Like you I search for ways
to say what remains
lumpen and inarticulate inside me.

Soon, any minute now, we will no longer
have something essential in common
despite our mingled cadre of tears.

This is a border zone. Here is
the line. Now you've crossed it.
If you can hear me, listen.

This is a dream that keeps coming.
You're a calf being born.
We reach for you, we knit together

your blood-slick ankles with our hands.
You hear four stomachs gurgling,
think, Mother, your music—

Every Boy, Every Blood

Sometimes we worship with guns.
Sometimes we need guns

to stand by us while we worship.
At dawn we killed the killers

then we washed our hands.
The clouds were like swimmers

dragging their arms across the sky.
Our dreams reassemble.

The fallow field, the shattered bridge,
each has its fragrant say.

Within these equations there's nothing
we can't calculate: my broken fingers

for your broken fingers, this anguish
for that face ten thousand rivers away.

My Eyes Were Harbors

Snowmelt makes the day a cloud
we peer through as if from the window

of an old plane. The plane is
our noontime bird, our daily reminder.

Time to reclaim the territories
rife with temporary flags.

For a moment I was no one's daughter,
nameless, a stranger suspended

in a stranger's care. I remember:
snowmelt turned the air.

I peered blindly, fingertips
my finest instruments,

lips my truest scales. I remember:
I was snow blind. I was swimming.

Small eras ended; others began.
I was suspended, snow blind

like any hungry bear in search of
seals or ice enough to stand:

just one hungry bear
swimming, swimming.

Rabbits with Wise Eyes

Pavel, Popper, do not abandon
what you've made. The rabbit
Michael belongs to you and no other.
Even when deer move among us
like dogs, their ruminant eyes remain.
Do not turn on them with the anger
of the half-rich who know what it is
to have a maid, but only on occasion.
What part of the mind speaks
to the part of the mind exploding
with pain? In the end you are not
exempt despite all the prices paid.
Raw skin toughens by degrees.
Sometimes we find what to cherish
without scarcity to teach us.
Because prey runs, we learn not to run,
not to turn our backs or look away
from the predator we dread and long
again to see because what we dread most
is it seeing us without being seen,
which is almost always the way.

The Famed Clipper Ship Is in Flames

Kissing is an experiment
we've already tried but
there remains more to learn.
We're amnesiacs.
We know and forget steadily
like a clock returning its hands
to move in circles across its face.
Once, the river ran red
with dye the factory let go.
Once, an assassin breached
the saffron gates. You appeared
without warning. I was a lamb
in a field, two and a half days.
Soon, a ship would carry us away.
A ship carried me here.

To Them Belong the Beds in Which We Sleep

The crowd's applause is no longer
linked to the action on the court

but to words on a giant screen
and images of themselves dancing.

The capitol is still where we keep
certain treasures, we still use

rivers to divide, but these days
the camouflage is bit-mapped.

That dog is an advanced weapons system
and he was the best soldier I've ever known.

Flocks of meals fall from the sky.
If you can hear them, it's too late.

Diorama

Hooves are stones
a body makes
a body borrows
to carry it from
shore to shore.
Minerals replace
minerals until
a body is a stone
and we learn all along
a body was a cast
a body was a mold
but we only learn it
after the mold is gone.
I no longer know
who stands beside me
though he has stood here
for a thousand years.
Our animals have
turned to stone. Still
they carry me or what
became me once
every cell was gone.

*

Aubade

This is how it is to sleep
with deer nearby, invisibly around
in beds of flattened grasses,
wet muzzles wetted with dew
late, when it comes,

and early they are standing,
true prey, watching the air
with satellite-dish ears as they nose
the ground, crushing ferns
between tooth and hoof.

Forgive me if I touch your face
in place of another face,
with these fingers in the place
of other fingers, my own,
the ones I remember.

There is no end that does not end,
no going on that does not worsen.
The moment is far away.
The dents in my eyes are
where the future lives

but my eyes are closed.
Sleep ravels away from me.
One by one we gentle our loves
to the ground. This is how
it is to sleep near a sea

that sounds like the traffic
of familiar feet, the way rain sounds
to the sea, the way deer sound
to a cougar gliding across the field
at hungry dawn.

Elegy

In a distant room
you are always dying.

We watch it come.
It comes slowly, in its way,

and with great speed.
In advance is like in retrospect:

past perfect, future perfect,
the imagined happening,

happening, happening.
Remove the visible world,

its crowds of guillemots
and auklets, its street signs

and stones. They promise
to offer less but longer.

We would take it but
in the end no offer is made.

There are measurements
too small to recognize,

imperatives too large to see.
All they find is a name.

Moonlight on the Strait of Juan
de Fuca finds night fish

and their glowing trails,
miniature Perseids in reverse.

As usual, cormorants
clean themselves bobbing

on the iron waves' sway.
What is in a name?

Your name is carried on
the tongues that taste you

searching for the right word
temporarily mislaid.

Elegy

Where does the will live?
In every cell. Where

the will to live? Every
cell. The bay is

ironclad, a smile
through trees.

Shuttered eyes
are hard closed.

Wind is nothing:
unseen, unheard.

An idea of return
blooms, a recidivist dream.

He is hovering.
He is released.

He is a light cloak
the air is wearing.

The bay does not
wish to be turned to.

The bay doesn't care
if you're on your knees.

Turn off the electric lights
in your little house.

Listen to the stupid birds
in their stupid trees.

Elegy

For days I feel you in the air
and I know exactly what to say.

I say, come back, come back
to your body, come back.

Everything is a constellation, but this
is the tethered length of a thought

because in the darkness I—
because in the breaking light I—

because there is a pair of small
leather gloves and a dozen triangle teeth

pressed into the road after
the rest of the animal is gone.

Elegy

It wasn't you,
the hummingbird

unexpectedly in the yard,
and it wasn't finding

what it was looking for either
skirting the empty tree.

A body by the river is a cliché,
but they found one

and cordoned off the road.
Newspapers remind us

we know more about decay
than we like to let on—

there are experts among us
who know death to the hour,

death by the degree. Then
there's what our own bodies tell us

day by day or sometimes
all of a sudden. The crime-scene

tape comes down. The parade-route
flags, the missing-person flyers,

the mourning cloths come down.
The sun sets differently by degrees

and again the river is a garden,
a mirrored highway for ruby-throats

with exacting coordinates
etched into their flight brains,

a gushing vein that feeds
and feeds the sea.

Elegy

We see how the children cluster
around the afflicted girl.

We're familiar with the way
cruelty accrues cruelty.

If we kept them, all our secret
diaries would read the same:

her blouse was high
and would be fun to unbutton,

ruffle listing to the left,
to the right.

All riders dismount.
All wrecks are transformed.

Which is the first fish
to inhabit the sunken cockpit?

How long before the fuselage is
a safe haven for anemones?

To render from memory
in memory the sail of a cheek

known first as electricity
in the brain then translated

into the fine movements of fingers
is an act of love

but in this crowded portrait room
let's forbid all graven images

let's respect in this way what
we love and cannot touch.

Vespers

In the long white corridor of birds
emptied of brains and stomachs
in the field or upon returning
dusted with arsenic and sewn up

again like fine evening clutches—
Athene blewitti, forest owlet,
willow warbler—you come to me
an apparition. Territory is

a patchwork of appointments,
of stumbled upon, of hiding,
of wishing to be found.
There is no category for things

that move more or less like wind.
Every stitch is a signature.
Every stitch is a constellation.
God begins at the end of your hand.

*

This Waking Life

Fish dart like birds flock.
Traffic runs like fish
hell-bent upstream.
We catch and release.
We cease. We forget.
We do it without noticing;
we put on our finest clothes.
We write love song after love
song and find it hurts most
when we stop singing.
The anchorwoman's hair
makes sense next to
the other anchorwoman's hair.
There are offices devoted
to the demise of old words,
others to the rise of new ones.
Routes are mapped.
Factories confuse the air.
From a footprint, experts can
construct a life story, predict
a future path. I don't want to
know who you are, I don't
want to tell you who I've been
walking down the street or
at night in my bed. I want to
sit next to you while fish kiss
and twist the birded surface
of the pond from underneath.

Different Habitats Make for Good Neighbors

If their tracks are any indication
the deer worship the yew,
filing from the woods
to circumambulate its spindly base.
Or something like that.
If hunger is a form of prayer.
If prayer is a means of vigilant
waiting. The yew shoulders
a burlap coat against the cold.
All night mirrors work their blind
eyes, pooling darkness, flashing
the occasional glare. If seeing is
a kind of faith. If faith is a type
of sustenance or at least a gesture
toward repair. Dawn arrives
smoothly, an ironness breathing
steam. The recklessly flying
thing, the unavoidable hazard
you walk right into is air.

I Saw a Brand-New Look

Truly now they are filling the sky with robotic eyes
with automaton dragonflies executing missions
named after homing pigeons wheeling twenty-five miles
in twenty-five minutes through artillery fire
and the long-eared mules they flew above
whose gift to warfare was steadiness pulling cannons
through snow. Probably it is useful to take occasionally
a bird's-eye view, to see ourselves moving as if on sped-up film
like ants through the colonies of their very long short lives.
We kept one self-contained in sand, sandwiched
between clear plastic walls. It arrived in the mail.
They were self-sufficient. I don't know if they were fed,
but surely if they required it by Mother they were
provided for just so like us all the years of that house.
They inhabited orderly the rooms they built;
they kept a graveyard chamber. One morning
we woke to one soldier left carrying inward all the dead
who surrounded him. I don't know how this relates
to what we call loyalty or love. I know that
of the approximately ten years' worth of books
immediately available to me about the social insects
Formicidae of the family Hymenoptera
I would happily delve into six months at least.
I don't know when and where ideas of loyalty and love
would arise in this literature of adaptation.
We hold in one hand a set of questions. We hold
in one hand a handful gleaned from sad experience.
For a time we are bewildered children. For a time
we are bewildered children dedicated to denying
we are bewildered. For a time we grow comfortable
with the fact that in the face of time we are destined
always to be bewildered. By then, bewilderingly,

we have a child of our own. First, the size of a pea,
the size of a lima bean, the size of a lime.
Finally, the size of the idea of a baby hammering away
with makeshift drumsticks on anything he can find.
Without music, life would be a mistake, Nietzsche
supposedly said. Right now I can't remember
if we approve or disapprove of Nietzsche
or if the Israeli Philharmonic has a stance on the matter
or if my mother does. Right now I'm standing naked
in a room filled with drumming, groping with my mouth
for small bites of time, but the cornfield outside
the window has been razed so to nothing I'm on view
but the occasionally passing mechanical eye.

Blast Harmonics

They weren't programmed to sleep.
One day in the laboratory
two of them stumbled accidentally
in midair and it was determined
the need for rest could be eliminated
by mapping a simple knocking pattern
onto their flight brains. This left
room for optional information.
They were taught horses are enormous.
Hummingbirds sound like giant fans.
Every nest has its weakling.
Every flower is a factory. They were
taught to buzz, to sting, to land.

The Queen Is Dead. Long Live the Queen.

I've been watching this bear for weeks.
At first it felt really intimate,
her fur pressed against the camera
and that little stick she chews
and one day cubs sort of mewing
all the time out of sight.
We were having what I thought of as
a really good day—I could see her
aristocratic profile and she seemed to be
taking more of an interest in the den—
when I noticed there were eleven
hundred and forty-three other people
watching her, too. It's true, we are particles
in a cloud of undifferentiated matter.
It's true, sometimes somewhere
in a small room a committee of strangers is
deciding your fate. I want to go home,
a boy whimpers from across the hall,
from his bear-filled room.

This Season It's All about 3D

I love my teeth and worry
about them lasting but in my coffin
they'll be what rises up toward you

in the dark. I've been working out.
I'm turning my natural weaknesses
into my most distinctive traits.

It pleases me to give you the answer
you hope to hear. I blame this
on my brain, its wired systems

of reward and release. All I want is
a voice to talk me through the night
from time to time when I wake

and can't remember the room.
Shine a lantern on your troubles,
the saying goes. But sometimes

everywhere it is light out.
Or lights out. Sometimes
everywhere it is raining.

Everyone moves through it
like hero-victims in a horror flick.
I can't see you, there you are.

Brainstorm

The portable scanners provide valuable information
but their glowing patterns present new questions

difficult to answer. Is such shimmering,
forlorn, Milky-Way-like, reserved for love

in memory alone? How completely
should we confuse another's scent with our own?

Outside, birds continue old habits of display.
Fanciers gather on rooftops, preferring the maps

pigeons stitch to air. Our methods differ but
fundamentally we agree. The future is made of secrets.

Every secret is a mission blinking like a ship lost at sea.
Find it. Find it. Find it. Then return.

Silver Whips of Trees

When the hail hits
the horses stand
close together.
We step outside.
We can't always tell
good fortune from bad.
When the air cracks
the leaves sign
a language surely
someone somewhere
can read. Not here.
A whinny stiffens
the wind. The horses
flare their nostrils,
pivot their feathered ears.
They call without moving.
They are next to one another
already, already right there.

When I Wake Too Soon

Every half hour the announcer
modulates his tone according to market
research on grandmothers listening
in nursing home increments: lavender tint,
lectures on Byzantium or vespers.
The possibilities for actionable distinction
are nearly infinite when you consider
a chair-bound constituency. If I consider
myself my doctor's employer, will that
change the diagnosis? Or the way
the paper feels against my skin
during the procedure, the parts I'm awake for,
that blurring out, that blurring in,
a latex glove against my cheek?
When the plane hits the wrong vector
there's no time to correct it but plenty of time
to crawl the news across the late-night screen,
to stop the presses so in the morning
the town's paperboys can deliver their own news.

Smaller Devices

Because my heart could not
contain you, it refused sympathy,

succor, news from anywhere.
Now it's as if a machine

records the feelings
I might have had.

Flashes like alarms
alert me, they're on file

should I wish to review them.
I don't. One was many

and became one again.
It was you I meant to belong to.

These bowing rituals never end.
All through me, seasons passing.

The late season grasses.
Lately, the grasses.

Theory of Correspondences

In the pasture
the guard llama blinks
to turn out the lights.
He readies himself
for another night
among sheep and
the coyote watch.
The moon pearls wool
and fence posts.
The sea lulls the sea
beneath the hill.
The wind is waking,
the wind is whispering,
this is your rocky shore.

Space Junk

There is a point on every mission
when something must be jettisoned

into the thin, black air.
Nothing likes to be abandoned,

no one likes to be compared.
There is a point when the plan

lifts from our control panels
and shimmers while we go ahead

and stare. How long do we
call the plan the plan after it

disappears? There's no such thing
as a few minutes alone. There's no

such thing as making up your mind
when everything is determined:

the rate of our turning, our distance
from the sun. I followed you here

with my naked eye. You've lost
your white glove. It travels now

like a comet burning up the sky.

About the Author

Lisa Olstein is the author of *Radio Crackling, Radio Gone,* winner of the 2005 Hayden Carruth Award, and *Lost Alphabet,* named one of the best poetry books of 2009 by *Library Journal. Little Stranger* is her third collection. She is the lyricist for the rock band Cold Satellite, fronted by Jeffrey Foucault, which has released two albums of songs based on her poems and lyrics: *Cold Satellite* (2010) and *Cavalcade* (2013). She is the recipient of a Pushcart Prize and fellowships from Centrum, the Massachusetts Cultural Council, and the Sustainable Arts Foundation. She cofounded and for ten years codirected the Juniper Initiative for Literary Arts & Action at the University of Massachusetts Amherst. She teaches in the New Writers Project, the MFA program based in the Department of English at University of Texas, Austin.

Lannan Literary Selections

For two decades Lannan Foundation has supported the publication
and distribution of exceptional literary works. Copper Canyon Press
gratefully acknowledges their support.

LANNAN LITERARY SELECTIONS 2013

Kerry James Evans, *Bangalore*

Sarah Lindsay, *Debt to the Bonesucking Snotflower*

Lisa Olstein, *Little Stranger*

Roger Reeves, *King Me*

Ed Skoog, *Rough Day*

RECENT LANNAN LITERARY SELECTIONS FROM
COPPER CANYON PRESS

James Arthur, *Charms Against Lightning*

Natalie Diaz, *When My Brother Was an Aztec*

Matthew Dickman and Michael Dickman, *50 American Plays*

Michael Dickman, *Flies*

Laura Kasischke, *Space, In Chains*

Deborah Landau, *The Last Usable Hour*

Michael McGriff, *Home Burial*

Heather McHugh, *Upgraded to Serious*

Valzhyna Mort, *Collected Body*

Tung Hui-Hu, *Greenhouses, Lighthouses*

Lucia Perillo, *Inseminating the Elephant*

John Taggart, *Is Music: Selected Poems*

Jean Valentine, *Break the Glass*

C.D. Wright, *One Big Self: An Investigation*

Dean Young, *Fall Higher*

For a complete list of Lannan Literary Selections from
Copper Canyon Press, please visit Partners on our Web site:
www.coppercanyonpress.org

Poetry is vital to language and living. Since 1972, Copper Canyon Press has published extraordinary poetry from around the world to engage the imaginations and intellects of readers, writers, booksellers, librarians, teachers, students, and donors.

WE ARE GRATEFUL FOR THE MAJOR SUPPORT PROVIDED BY:

THE PAUL G. ALLEN
FAMILY FOUNDATION

THE MAURER FAMILY
FOUNDATION

NATIONAL
ENDOWMENT
FOR THE ARTS

WASHINGTON STATE
ARTS COMMISSION

Anonymous

Arcadia Fund

John Branch

Diana and Jay Broze

Beroz Ferrell & The Point, LLC

Mimi Gardner Gates

Gull Industries, Inc.
on behalf of William and Ruth True

Mark Hamilton and Suzie Rapp

Carolyn and Robert Hedin

Steven Myron Holl

Rhoady and Jeanne Marie Lee

Maureen Lee and Mark Busto

New Mexico Community Foundation

H. Stewart Parker

Penny and Jerry Peabody

Joseph C. Roberts

Cynthia Lovelace Sears and Frank Buxton

The Seattle Foundation

Charles and Barbara Wright

The dedicated interns and faithful
volunteers of Copper Canyon Press

To learn more about underwriting Copper Canyon Press titles,
please call 360-385-4925 ext. 103

The Chinese character for poetry is made up of two parts:
"word" and "temple." It also serves as pressmark for
Copper Canyon Press.

The poems are set in Sabon.
Book design and composition by Phil Kovacevich.
Printed on archival-quality paper at McNaughton & Gunn, Inc.